I0606295

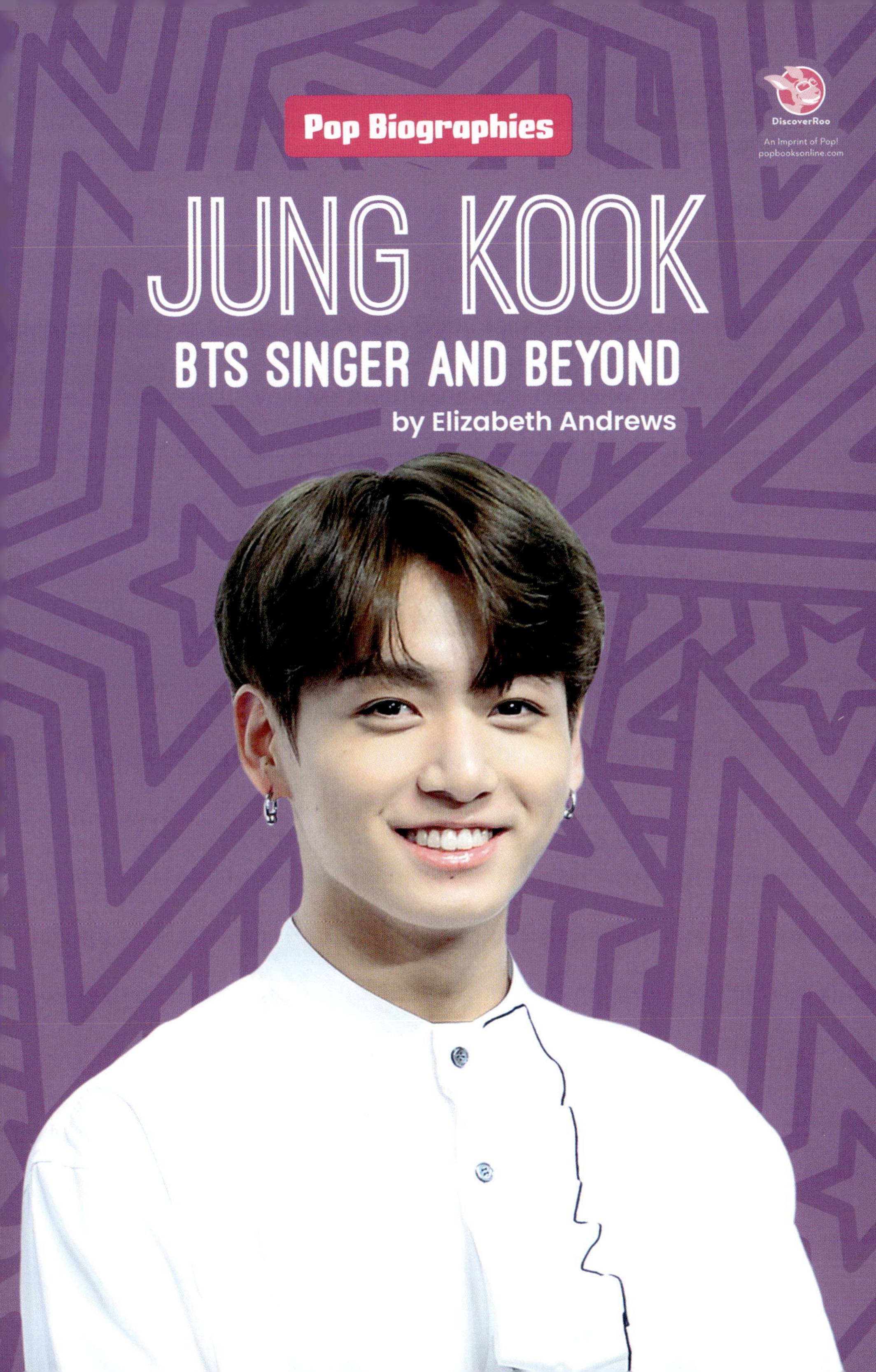
Pop Biographies
JUNG KOOK
BTS SINGER AND BEYOND
by Elizabeth Andrews
DiscoverRoo
An Imprint of Pop!
popbooksonline.com

WELCOME TO DiscoverRoo!

This book is filled with videos, puzzles, games, and more! Scan the QR codes* while you read, or visit the website below to make this book pop.

popbooksonline.com/kook

abdobooks.com

Published by Pop!, a division of ABDO, PO Box 398166, Minneapolis, Minnesota 55439.

Printed in the United States of America, North Mankato, Minnesota.

052023
082023

Cover Photo: Getty Images
Interior Photos: Getty Images, Shutterstock Images
Editor: Grace Hansen
Series Designer: Colleen McLaren

Library of Congress Control Number: 2022950558

Publisher's Cataloging-in-Publication Data

Names: Andrews, Elizabeth, author.
Title: Jung Kook: BTS singer and beyond / by Elizabeth Andrews
Other title: BTS singer and beyond
Description: Minneapolis, Minnesota : Pop!, 2024 | Series: Pop biographies | Includes online resources and index
Identifiers: ISBN 9781098244378 (lib. bdg.) | ISBN 9781098245078 (ebook)
Subjects: LCSH: Jungkook, 1997- --Juvenile literature. | BTS (Musical group)--Juvenile literature. | K-pop (Music)--Juvenile literature. | Singers--Juvenile literature.
Classification: DDC 782.42166092--dc23

*Scanning QR codes requires a web-enabled smart device with a QR code reader app and a camera.

TABLE OF CONTENTS

CHAPTER 1

BEFORE BOY BAND

Jeon Jung-kook was born on September 1, 1997, in Busan, South Korea. Busan is the second largest city in South Korea. Jung Kook grew up with his mom, dad, and older brother.

WATCH A VIDEO HERE!

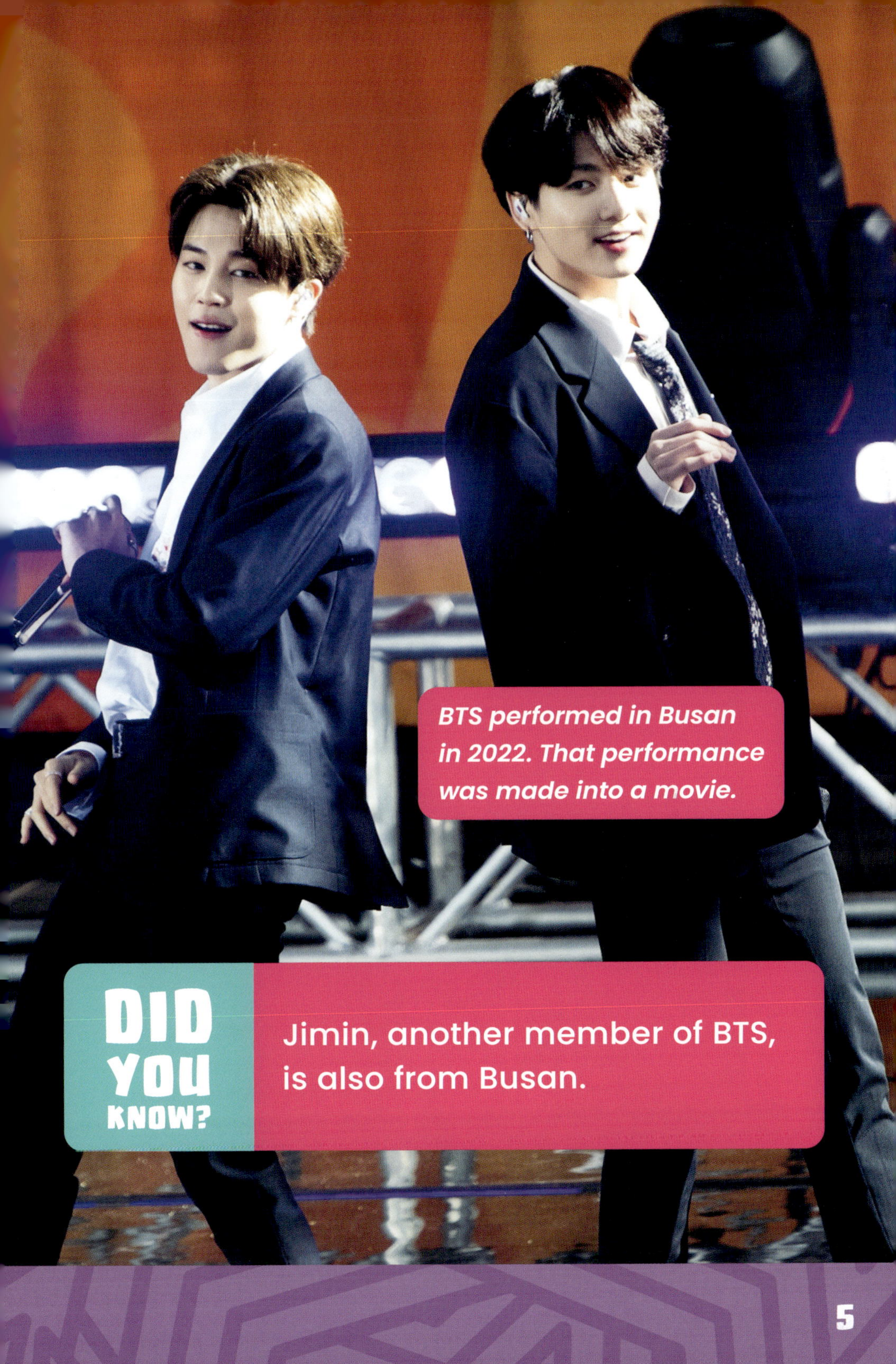

BTS performed in Busan in 2022. That performance was made into a movie.

DID YOU KNOW?

Jimin, another member of BTS, is also from Busan.

When he was young, Jung Kook wanted to be a **badminton** player. But after he saw the famous K-pop rapper G-Dragon perform, he decided he wanted to be a singer. In 2011, Jung Kook tried out for the South Korean talent show *Superstar K*. He didn't win, but

G-Dragon is also a fashion designer.

RM's full name is Kim Nam-joon.

he did catch the attention of several entertainment companies.

Jung Kook chose to join Big Hit Entertainment after he saw future bandmate RM rap. RM was **signed** to Big Hit. Jung Kook knew he wanted to be there too!

Jung Kook speaks Korean, Japanese, and some English.

Jung Kook was only 13 when he started working to become a K-pop **idol**. In South Korea, a performer at this stage of their career is called a trainee. Jung Kook learned a lot. Big Hit Entertainment sent him to Los Angeles in 2012 for dance training. They wanted him at his best when he officially joined BTS in 2013!

Jung Kook went to school in Busan. But when he moved to Seoul to train with Big Hit, he switched to a school there. In 2014 he started high school at the School of Performing Arts Seoul (SPAS).

Jung Kook said he was inspired by Justin Bieber.

CHAPTER 2

BTS BEGINS

A **producer** from Big Hit Entertainment began putting together the band that would become BTS in 2010. Band members were picked for their singing, dancing, and rapping skills.

LEARN MORE HERE!

BTS's style has changed over the years. In the band's early days they wore a lot of jewelry.

Jung Kook is the maknae. In K-pop "maknae" refers to the youngest member of the group. Jung Kook's bandmates were there for many important moments. They even attended his graduation in 2017!

BTS MEMBERS

Big Hit Entertainment was small. But they took good care of the boys and were passionate about BTS's success. Before their debut on June 12, 2013, promotion material was released introducing each band member to the public.

Jung Kook sings, raps, and dances in BTS. His group members and fans call him their Golden Maknae! They say that he is good at everything he does.

DID YOU KNOW?

Jung Kook is also talented at drawing, filmmaking, and tae kwon do.

BTS released their first collection of **singles** called *2 Cool 4 Skool* in 2013. They followed it up with their first full album *Dark & Wild* in 2014. After that, their image changed from dark and edgy to down-to-earth and meaningful.

Jung Kook was shy when he started out in BTS. As the band's popularity grew, so did his confidence.

For their US TV debut, BTS performed at the 2017 American Music Awards (AMAs).

The Most Beautiful Moment in Life, Pt. 1 and *Pt. 2* were released in 2015. BTS's popularity grew. They went on a world tour and *Pt. 2* topped **charts** in six countries. Jung Kook had a solo song on the 2016 *Wings* album called "Begin."

The BTS boys make finger hearts by crossing their thumb and pointer finger.

In the following years, each BTS release ranked higher and higher on global charts. Singles from the *Love Yourself* trilogy went **platinum**, won awards, and broke records BTS already had set. Classic BTS songs like "Euphoria," "Mic Drop," and "DNA" became popular around the world. The band members believe their fans, who are called the ARMY, are the reason BTS has been so successful.

THE BTS EFFECT

The Bangtan Universe (BU) is a pretend world created by Big Hit Entertainment. Each member plays a character in the universe. Their stories are told through content like music, videos, short films, mobile games, books, and webtoons set in the BU. Fans pay a lot of attention to all content released so they can follow along with the story.

CHAPTER 3

TAKING OVER THE WORLD

BTS has continued to meet and go beyond their original goals. **Dominating** the American music scene was in reach. When "Boy with Luv" featuring Halsey was released in 2019, it broke the YouTube record for most viewed video in 24 hours. The song also won 12 different music awards!

EXPLORE LINKS HERE!

BTS and Halsey performed "Boy with Luv" at the 2019 Billboard Music Awards.

Jung Kook and his bandmates appeared on more screens every day. The pressure of being such a big star can be a lot to deal with. Jung Kook has said he worries about disappointing fans. But he is determined to stay true to himself no matter how many eyes are on him.

BTS fans have assigned each member a cartoon character that best describes them. Jung Kook is a bunny.

When COVID-19 changed BTS's tour plans, they decided to try to make their mark in the United States.

The next set of releases was titled *Map of the Soul. Persona* was released on April 19, 2019, and 7 hit the **charts** on February 21, 2020. The album debuted at #1 on the Billboard 200 chart. Sadly, the COVID-19 **pandemic** forced BTS to cancel their Map of the World tour.

The pandemic didn’t slow down Jung Kook and BTS entirely. The band performed virtual concerts and spoke at graduation events. “Dynamite” was released on August 21, 2020. It blew

The Grammys is one of the most respected music award ceremonies worldwide.

up and reached #1 on Billboard Hot 100 immediately. "Dynamite" earned a Grammy nomination. BTS released *BE* in November. It was an inspirational album for the world during a troubling time.

CHAPTER 4

NEW ADVENTURES

In 2021 BTS released yet another English hit. "Butter" was the longest running #1 song on the Billboard Hot 100. And it was nominated for a Grammy. Once again, BTS overtook records they had already set!

COMPLETE AN ACTIVITY HERE!

Jung Kook and his bandmates were some of the most popular faces in entertainment. They worked with big names like McDonald's and Louis Vuitton. The Permission to Dance World Tour sold out. Fans were excited to see the boys live again.

BTS came up with new hand gestures to promote their single "Butter."

After the world tour, BTS told fans they would be taking a break. Some boys had to join the South Korean military while others were ready to work on solo projects. All of them were tired from **constantly** releasing music and performing.

BTS visited President Joe Biden at the White House in May 2022.

Jung Kook began working on his own solo music, determined to see where his career could go. Speaking about the break he said, "We're each going to take some time to have fun and experience new things."

Jung Kook performed "Dreamers" at the World Cup opening ceremony in Qatar.

After announcing the break, Jung Kook released a **single** called "Left and Right" with Charlie Puth. He also thrilled fans with the FIFA World Cup song

"Dreamers." His BTS bandmates encouraged him to write and release even more.

Jung Kook and BTS have made many incredible accomplishments. The non-English speaking musical group took over the world! BTS's music breaks down barriers between languages and people.

Jung Kook earned the nickname "Sold Out King" for always selling out items he uses and wears.

MAKING CONNECTIONS

TEXT-TO-SELF

Do you listen to BTS? If so, what is your favorite song and why? If not, what album would you be most interested in listening to?

TEXT-TO-TEXT

Have you read any books about musicians from outside the United States? If so, how were they similar to or different from Jung Kook and the boys from BTS?

TEXT-TO-WORLD

Why do you think people from all different places and cultures love BTS so much?

GLOSSARY

badminton — a sport that uses rackets to hit a shuttlecock (also called a birdie) over a net.

chart — a ranking of music (songs or albums) according to popularity during a given period of time.

constantly — continuously over a period of time.

dominate — rising above.

idol — one who is loved and respected to a great degree.

pandemic — a disease outbreak that spreads to many countries.

platinum — a single or album that has sold one million copies or more.

producer — the person or company that makes something. Music producers put songs together.

signed — agreed legally to make music for one person or company.

single — a song that is released as a stand-alone from an album.

INDEX

DiscoverRoo!
ONLINE RESOURCES

This book is filled with videos, puzzles, games, and more! Scan the QR codes* while you read, or visit the website below to make this book pop.

popbooksonline.com/kook

*Scanning QR codes requires a web-enabled smart device with a QR code reader app and a camera.